FOOTNOTES ON A LANDSCAPE

PART 1

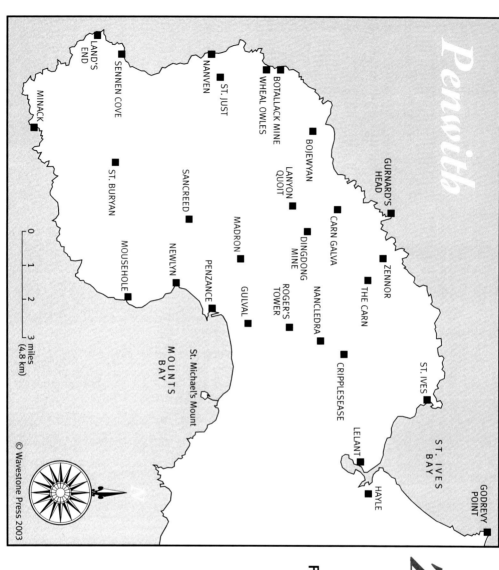

Zawn Leno

WORDS & IMAGES
FROM WEST CORNWALL

BY DAVID WHITTAKER

Published by

wavestone press

www.wavestonepress.co.uk

'Walking, the feet are informed' Peter Lanyon

Footnotes on a Landscape – 1

Zawn Lens

WORDS & IMAGES
FROM WEST CORNWALL

DAVID WHITTAKER

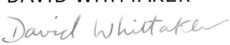

wavestone
press

This book is dedicated to the tender memory of my mother Mona (1927-2002)
– in boundless gratitude for crates of stout, spud cakes & giving me the chance.

Zawn Lens: Words & Images from West Cornwall
ISBN: 0-9545194-0-X
Copyright © David Whittaker 2003
Wavestone Press
6 Rochester Place, Charlbury, Oxon OX7 3SF
Tel. 01608-811858
Email: books@whithew.freeserve.co.uk
www.wavestonepress.co.uk

ACKNOWLEDGEMENTS

I particularly want to thank the following people for their patience, encouragement and generosity of spirit:

Willie Barns-Graham; Andrew & Martin Lanyon; Jane & the late Tony O'Malley; Dr Roger Slack; Michael & Margaret Snow; Sarah Stoten; Wendy Wilson; and Monica Wynter for extra tuition & intuition.

For providing nutritious succour for both body and mind and a bullet-proof refuge from the Cornish elements thanks are due to Joy & Ray Kell of Gurnard's Head Hotel and Sue & the late John Wilson of Tregeraint House, Zennor.

The wise counsel of Jan Beare & Craig Weatherhill rescued me from vanishing without trace into the yawning zawn of Cornish place-names.

Keith Rigley's mouse clicking hand provided essential guidance through the brave new world (new to me) of publishing technology – cheers chap.

A shorter version of Tony O'Malley's obituary appeared in *The Guardian*.

The genesis of this venture owes something to the bountiful and stimulating company of Jillian and Graham Binns. Their deaths, within days of each other, leave me with a heavy heart as this book goes to press.

And the last shall be first: my wife Penny and daughter Alice are a constant source of delight, good humour and forbearance (not to mention skilful proof reading), keeping me on the right side of *compos mentis* – just. They are the still centre of my life's erratic orbit.

60 copies of Zawn Lens have been signed and numbered, with an additional print for subscribers.

Printed by Headland Printers, Penzance

CONTENTS

BOTALLACK

A crowning achievement
defiant of the deafening,
thunderous sea.

Mine of wonder, mine of glory,
an adventurer's story granted
the stamp of royal approval.

Its engine beam pumped
and fuelled an empire of dreams
from steaming portals

submerged and descending
the adamantine depths of hell
subdued below a ceiling of sea.

Desolate and bereft of ore,
a backdrop to romantic lore
it endures, resolutely engraved
against a molten sea.

CARN
GALVA

At prey in plumes of grace
    the startled swoop
        defines a parabolic space

        Sideways dart the winds of change
    a sudden sweep
expands its awful range

Uplift flight from crow's defence
    an aerial curve
        refines the savage elegance

        With deadly focused poise
    a single final dive
concludes its game without a noise

SANCREED

Well-dressed offerings in rags,
gnarled and animated with
doleful garlands of hope,
this saintly place of raucous rooks
and a forgotten saint
sanctified by shabby icons from
well-wishing devotees:

    a fetish of feathers and bent key-rings,
    that once cherished one-eyed teddy bear,
    motley coloured ribbons and bows,
    a severed ponytail terminally braided,
    glass jars opaque with implication,
    corn dollies unseasonal and sullied,
    and a somewhat seemingly inapt
    kind of wooden Polynesian idol.
    Perhaps all gods are equally welcome
    here in this sanative place?

Descend these seven ponderous
well-trodden steps of velvety moss,
inhale the moist subterranean
mystery to a solution and
exhale spring-healed from
this saintly place of raucous rooks
and a forgotten saint.

Votive offerings by Sancreed holy well

Merrymaid

Bench end wench
    With scaly tail
Combs the waves
    With her siren's wail

Mathey Trewhella's song
    Of such sweet voice
Seals his fate and
    Becomes her choice

Down Pendour Cove
    Entranced in her glass
She beds her love
    As he gasps his last

Bench end wench
    With scaly tail
Combs the waves
    With her siren's wail

ZENNOR

His breath's a vapor & his life's a fpan
T'is glorious mifrey to be born a man

Zennor
>   Where the Quick are the dead
>   And the Berrymans rest
>   Punningly beneath the soil
>   Overlooked by Heron's Nest

>   Where the cow once ate the bell
>   Rope, Guernseys' udder swagger
>   Fills the evening air with smells,
>   Bells and lowing clamour

>   Where a petulant Lawrence
>   Took his Red Baron Frieda,
>   He met with xenophobia and
>   Had nowhere left to hide her

Zennor
>   Where the goats are coy,
>   And with local charm
>   You can sink your joy
>   In a pint of tinner's gloom

His breath's a vapor & his life's a fpan
T'is glorious mifrey to be born a man

(This verse opens and closes with an inscription from a Zennor tombstone)

Zennor

Zennor

MORRAB LIBRARY

Amid the dehumidifying
Gentle hum of books
Laughter sprinkles the musty
Air to steal silent looks

This collected collection
Of volumes do furnish a room
The frayed cosy opulence
Of a tome-lined womb

Exotic gardens encroach
Via sunny window frames
Magnolia gloriosa, *Grandiflora*
And more inscrutable Latin names

Arcane gossip is scattered by
A rousing bygone phone
Reverberating wall to wall
Its nostalgic ringing tone

The Jenner Room is the locus
For all Cornubian research
From wreckers, fogous and piskies
To the life of Lamorna Birch

Raiding the pantry is such
A highlight (at least it is for me)
The thrilling anticipation of
Bourbon creams dunked in tea

Napoleonic memorabilia
Spills out of crannies and nooks
Amid the dehumidifying
Gentle hum of books

SMEATON'S PIER

Night harbour hush

Even The Sloop is serene

Orion's Belt clarifies

A cryptic canvas sky

Sweepingly stretched

Above this terraced town

So easy on the cubist eye

Anchored in space

Lightly bobbing on infinitude

A nimbus moon attends

The sea's sad sigh

Godrevy's cautionary arc

Blinks reassurance as

Wharf waves lap the

Night harbour hush

Zennor, near The Carn

HIGH COUNTRY

'drawing organises your looking' Bryan Wynter

    A gentle man (by all accounts)
        A gentle conscientious man
    An outsider probing an interior
        Winding stream

(And the curlews' flutings
saved the day
– or so they say)

    Carn man whose home is at home
        Nestled in elemental rock-pile
    'Approaching nature from the other side'
        On firestreaked moors

    Kayak man at swim in oils
        A riverbed romantic whose
    Fluid confluence of hand and eye
        Ingrained the blue deep canvas

(But also gothic raven man
with spiky beak and talons honed)

    A recessive space man, where
        Images move out of concave enclaves
    To reflect stately mirages
        Drawn from terrestrial shadows

    Late man of Zennor
        Still in his seedtime
    A gentle man (by all accounts)
        A gentle conscientious man

(And the curlews' flutings
saved the day
– or so they say)

           For Jillian and Graham Binns

Abandoned quarried block, Zennor

Zennor, near The Carn

BARNOON

through a
spy glass
picture this

      glazed grave at rest
      on summit slope
      a tomb with a view
      to die for

      within scene unheard
      of the once yielding sea
      the once providing sea

      from point of clodgy
      permit a naive eye
      to surf the great cove's
      tidal arc to island chapel
      where for company
      adjacent godrevy renders
      a stone warning

      within sight unsound
      of the once fatal sea
      the once wrecking sea

      gaze awhile upon
      the primitive potter's
      grave kiln toil of
      monumental modesty
      its old iron oxide
      brushed and fired to
      speck burst tinge

into these hands
from poorhouse
deliverance came
lapsed salvationist
mariner and artist
a fish shaped soul
without knowing it

his ubiquitous lighthouse
makes a last stand
and welcomes the
watery eyed voyager
on a stairway
to haven's beacon
on this tomb with a view

of the 'what-used-to-be' sea
but for now is a pleasure
leisurewear sea

through a
spy glass
picture this

Giew Mine, Cripplesease

Detail of Leach tile on Alfred Wallis's grave

WHEAL
OWLES

Deadly, the lure of the east-west vein
Veers past land's edge in a flood of pain

Skeletal vestiges, bones of toil,
Gaunt shadows on a wounded soil

The cry, the lonely cry of the gull

Houses of water echo fathomless grief
Down sunless galleries lacking relief

The sea's implacable torrent of abuse
Exacts a grave price without a truce

The cry, the lonely cry of the wind

Tears blend lament in a seam of sorrow
Prayers beseech that tomorrow and tomorrow

The innocents emerge from their choking plight
To ascend to grass and breathe the light

The cry, the forsaken cry of the boy

Part of Wheal Owles sett

LETTER TO
W. S. GRAHAM

(please forward to wheneverwhere)

Dear Sydney,
How goes it scotch man
on the other side of language?
I do so hope you don't think it
too impertinent of me implementing
your favoured epistolary form
(try saying that after a dram or three),
but your tone seems to me to invite a like response
and there's a few things I'd like to address
to the front of your face
while I'm in the mood.

(By the way, the foxgloves' digitalis
were brilliant this year in the late Zennor spring)

I would just like to thank you so very much indeed
for breaking the sound barrier
with your silent syntax.
It's not so much what you say
as how you say you become.
You allowed the language to sound you
and you knew your place;
that place spoke you,
simply said not meant simply.
You speak therefore we are.

(Oh yes, while I remember, your timeless university at Trevaylor
is now a care home for the third age of forgetting)

What ye did was a rare thing Joke Grim:
you managed to abstract the obstacles
from your life sentence and the words
became their own metaphor;
you drew clusters of artists, you see,
who saw not so much what you say
as how you say you become.
And your breath distilled
the ear's acoustic space.
We listen therefore you are.

(And by the by, over at Churchtown Madron in
the William IV the one-armed bandits
have proliferated, nudge-nudge, and alas,
the vinegar outsmells the ale.
Also, you should see Mount View, dear Mount View
where you crossed the final threshold, it's now looking
washed whiter than whitewashed white)

Finally, I do apologise for keeping you,
I'd just like to say that this you knew:
the act of reading rewrites the writer's art of
right reading.

I'll now shut up.

It goes without saying, should you ever be passing
our way do give us a tap.

Cheerio,

A fellow howling Gael.

P. S. I do often wonder are you below in steerage? Or did you,
maimed as you were for the job, somehow qualify for the upper
deck? Either way I hope there's a decent ruddy bar.
See ye whereverwhen.

Nanven

Nanven

NANVEN

And the attentive seal is watching me.
  He's watching me watching him
  watching me attending to a banana.

In this time carved place carved of curved space,
  glaring white on beach-bleached white,
  horizon's disc rim shimmers the naked eye
  into conjured regions decked in sunken fable.
  A phalanx of urgent waves is time's
  keen tool for this curvaceous place,
  dimly burnished by excessive caress.
  (Overhead cirrus whispers relief
  upon a bejewelled sea.)

And, again, what is that dull sort of boom?
  It seems to come from inside the ear.
  Do seals have ears?
  He's still watching – I'm not,
  at least I was taught it's rude to stare.

Slow motion moulded
  liquid aeons of all our yesterdays
  crystallise time's trajectory in
  this nest of primeval eggs,
  grooved and scoured
  by the moon's interminable
  waning, waxing and cascading
  game of tide and time
  (and hide and seek).

And the seal has disappeared,
  I can't blame him.
  Mind how you go old son.

FIGMENT

Faceless
groping liquid curves,
    the emergent anonymity
takes hold of potent form

IS THIS THE WAY OUT OR THE WAY IN?

Sightless
lusty shifting shades
    gratify an itch to conjugate
in the birth of dissolution

HAVEN'T I BEEN YOU SOMEWHERE BEFORE?

Soundless
mutating dreams of vapour
    gesture forth
a zone of hazy sinews

ONE RUMP OR TWO?

Genderless
a private loss penetrates
    an absence in the
incessant play of form

YOUR SPACE OR MINE?

For Colin Scott

Morning Wind on the Cornfield – July 1966 by Tony O'Malley.
Mixed media on paper 67 x 52 (private collection)

THE LOOM OF SONG

He searches winter
    by the stark eye
of the wheeling hawk.
    He searches twilight
by the ruling owl's
    hypnotic orbs.
He searches for her hand,
    the tender hand that
weaves autumn colours
    from the loom of song.

With speechless stare
    he listens for colour,
below the modest mantled
    breast of Slievenamon.
As twilight transmutes
    the score of fading day
he listens for a tumble of
    crows, a reassuring
assembly of caws
    by the conference tree.

(And do you remember
The morning wind on the cornfield?
Its spiral torque stirred and set
To motion as in the falcon's gyre,
Do you recall that summer's day?
Was it on Ding Dong, Trevaylor,
Or some other Scilly place?
I wish I knew.)

Unseen, he searches.
    The twinkle in the
darkly bright
    eye of the *Saoi*
illumines the sombre
    Samhain sky.
The eye that knows
    its own inscape
by the scope of
    seasonal change.

Their hands dovetail
    in a fondly-firm
firmly-gentle grip,
    as their love sails
from the loom of song.
    Nearby, the stringless harp
silently awaits, silently awaits
    the spring renewal and
redemptive stations
    of Good Friday's grace.

For Jane O'Malley

KITE

The rates of growth and form begin
As wheels of colour whirl and spin.

Chromatic fugue's vibrant hue
Of olive, vermilion or cobalt blue
Impels the eye to mimic and dance
The gestures and cadence of chance.

Glacial topologies splinter and melt
Where wind on burning wind is felt,
In golden celebration of fire
Geometries of colour fuel the pyre.

Kaleidoscopic things of a kind
Correspond from mind to mind,
Wave upon wave's economy of line
Ebb and flow tracing design.

As the colour roulette bursts with vivacity
Regenerations of growth unfold for infinity.

For Wilhelmina Barns-Graham's
90th birthday

LELANT

DANGER – GOLF
KEEP TO PATH
(sign near the churchyard)

Late October sun on
bleached hollow
snail shell.

(The gentle clack
of golf balls)

A fat rabbit sits,
as an ornate urn,
perfectly still.

(Adjoining holes
one & fourteen)

Headstones cast
sundial shadows on
fellow headstones.

(The loud thwack
of golf balls)

A fat rabbit can be
stunningly quick,
like a bloody golf ball.

SILENT
FLIGHT

*'The air is a very definite world of activity as complex
and demanding as the sea ...' Peter Lanyon*

Grounded
in vertiginous
flights
of fancy,
winging the
weathered
edge of
giddy speed
(he had the sky in his belly).
Piloting
nervous visions
in the race of space
to a climate of change,
tilting and
catching the
barren lands
by surprise,
a pause of
coastal silence
soothes a
restless cold pool
of warm light
(he had the sky in his belly).

A Flotsam of Footnotes
to the Poems

These notes may appear totally superfluous to some locals.

However, I know from the experience of talking to people further afield (i.e., east of the Tamar, even east of the Hayle!) that many of the characters and places mentioned in this book are unfamiliar.

I also happen to like composing notes and the opportunity they provide to explore some of the more peripheral byways of life.

Botallack

Mining has gone on here since at least the early 18th century.

By the late 19th century the works extended for over a mile out *under* the Atlantic, the sea running red from the mineral deposits.

Queen Victoria visited in 1846, indicating the importance of this mine to the industrial revolution. In 1865 the Prince and Princess of Wales (later Edward VII and Queen Alexandra) made a descent into the depths of the mine in a 'gig'. This started a trend and people travelled from all over the country via the newly opened Paddington to Penzance railway to do likewise (demonstrating that the fad-setting influence of the cult of celebrity is nothing new). The mine, very sensibly, started charging half a guinea for the pleasure.

Botallack means 'Talek's ('big browed') dwelling'.

Carn Galva

Having clambered to the top of Carn Galva ('lookout rockpile'), the second highest point in West Penwith, I sat quietly eating my pasty observing the art of a peregrine falcon in quest of its own lunch.

Sancreed

This parish takes its name possibly from St Credan. Not far from the main church there is the site of an ancient chapel and holy well. It's uncertain to whom they were originally dedicated, but to this day the folklore surrounding wells and springs remains potent. Anthropologists have named this particular fascination 'hydrophilia' (they would).

MERRYMAID

Somewhere in W. S. Graham's letters he says that a mermaid is an impossible subject for a poem. Having written this verse (inspired by the 500 year old carving in Zennor church) I now agree with Graham!

It has been said that behind every mermaid story there lies a seal.

ZENNOR

The churchyard in Zennor makes for an incomparable terminus to have one's mortal coil interred, surrounded by moors, rock formations, field patterns and the Atlantic ocean. Two of the most frequent local names to recur on the tombstones are Quick and Berryman.

In March 1916 D. H. Lawrence and his German wife Frieda (having initially stayed at The Tinners Arms) moved into nearby Higher Tregerthen cottage at a rent of £5 per year. He referred to the area as the 'promised land'. With the world at war they were treated with much suspicion. This suspicion intensified when the couple started singing German songs and it was claimed that lights were glimpsed through the blackout curtains. This was taken to be a signal to submarines out at sea.

The fact that Frieda was related to Baron von Richthofen, the Red Baron, definitely didn't help matters and in October 1917 the police delivered a court injunction ordering them out of the Duchy.

While here Lawrence wrote a good deal of *Women in Love*.

MORRAB LIBRARY

This is a large, independent library uniquely located in Morrab Gardens in Penzance. Founded in 1818 it moved to Morrab House in 1889. As so many people referred to it as the Morrab Library, that became its name in 1997. As well as a substantial store of various books, more than 40,000, it happens to house one of the world's biggest Napoleonic collections.

The atmosphere is, fittingly, as pleasantly unique as its location.

Morrab comes from the Cornish *morrep* meaning 'seaboard'.

Smeaton's Pier

The pier in St Ives was first built by Smeaton in 1770 and further extended in 1890. The granite blocks were quarried from the moors above Zennor and transported by sea.

Godrevy is the lighthouse immortalised in Virginia Woolf's novel *To the Lighthouse*.

High Country

A homage to the painter Bryan Wynter (1915–1975).

Sven Berlin has told how Wynter, looking down on Zennor and feeling suicidal, suddenly noticed the curlews flying overhead making their fluting calls in the moonlight. Life seemed worthwhile again and he painted *Birds Disturbing the Sleep of a Town* (1948). Berlin's stories are often tinged by a petite dash of poetic licence.

Wynter had an enthusiasm for punning, a condition he shared with Sydney Graham, and the following translingual conundrum is a typical example (provided by Graham Binns): *PAS DE LEUR RHÔNE QU'A NOUS*.

Barnoon

It was on August 29 1942 that Madron Workhouse lost its most celebrated inmate. Artist and mariner Alfred Wallis died here of 'senile decay' after an at times frustrating sojourn of 14 months. Wallis's remains were rescued from the pitiful ignominy of a pauper's grave by the pecuniary intervention of Adrian Stokes, who paid the Salvation Army £4.10/- for a plot in Barnoon cemetery in St Ives (high up behind what is now the Tate Gallery, but was then the gasworks). It is one of the harsh ironies of art history that at this time Wallis had work hanging in the Museum of Modern Art in New York (donated by Nicholson). Sometime later Bernard Leach designed and made the tiled monument. Wallis's date of birth on the memorial is incorrect: it reads August 18, instead of August 8 1855.

The Workhouse, also known as the Poorhouse, later became a care home for the elderly before being turned into a slaughterhouse (for animals).

Barnoon means 'summit of the down'.

WHEAL OWLES

The Wheal Owles ('cliff mine') sett of mines are located just south of Botallack. It was here on Thursday, January 10 1893 that an underground chamber, 85 fathoms down (about 500 feet), was flooded, due to a magnetic dialling error, with the loss of 19 men and a boy. Their remains were never recovered.

LETTER TO W. S. GRAHAM

For about 40 years the peripatetic poet Sydney Graham was associated with Cornwall (1951–1956 were spent away):

1943–1946   Germoe, a caravan (named 'Wheelhouse');

1947–1949   Mevagissey (though a good deal of '48 was spent in New York);

1950   July to September, Zennor, The Carn, while Bryan Wynter was away, then until December, Truro & Perranporth hospitals (having fallen 30 feet from a roof, at a party in St Ives, he had his smashed kneecap removed. Acknowledging his luck he said 'I have angels galore awatching over me');

1956–1962   Begins '56 with Alan Lowndes in Back Road West, St Ives; then at Sven Berlin's cottage at Cripplesease named 'Penderleath' (now the Cripplesease pottery) before settling with Nessie (he had married Nessie Dunsmuir in 1954) at Gurnard's Head coastguard cottage in March, where they stayed until 1962. During these years WSG did occasional auxiliary coastguard work from a hut at the tip of the Head. (Nessie would watch Sydney's glowing lantern gradually disappear down the track across the fields.) The base can still be seen, but many years ago the hut itself was officially dispensed with and pushed into the sea. Graham, never one for false humility, described himself as the brain of Gurnard's Head;

1962–1967   Trevaylor near Gulval; settles in the lodge opposite Trevaylor which he called 'Woodfield' (Trevaylor is a large country house and grounds. Between 1962 and 1972 it was owned by the painter and patron Nancy Wynne-Jones. She had bought it from 'Old Mrs Brooke Bond Tea', as the tea heiress Miss Hooper was locally known. The house provided studio space for many artists including Bryan Wynter and Tony O'Malley who described the stimulus of this 'colony' as a kind of university. It subsequently became a guest house and is currently a retirement home);

1967–1986   Madron, Mount View cottage. Graham died here, of cancer, on January 9 1986.

Nanven

Situated at the mouth of Cot Valley, this is an area of great geological interest. Written records of mining in the vicinity exist going back to Tudor times.

On certain days the Isles of Scilly, 28 miles away, can be faintly detected without the assistance of a telescopic appliance.

The curious deep boom that recurs every afternoon turns out to be Concorde, somewhere in the upper stratosphere, breaking the sound barrier as it heads out towards the New World.

Nanven is from the Cornish *gwyn* meaning 'white'.

Figment

The painter Colin Scott, who has lived in Penzance for over 20 years, asked me to write something in response to his work. The human figure, prominent in his art, is always presented in a somewhat amorphous, nebulous state suggesting the ageless theme of metamorphosis.

The Loom of Song

An elegy for Tony O'Malley.

Irish references in the poem:

- Slivenamon is the mountain overlooking the O'Malley home. This is the Anglicised spelling of *Sliabh na mBan* – meaning 'mountain of the women'.
- *Saoi* means 'wise man' and is pronounced 'see'.
- *Samhain* means 'November' (it can also mean 'Halloween') and is pronounced 'sow-an' (sow rhyming with cow).

Kite

Wilhelmina Barns-Graham was born in 1912 in St Andrews, Scotland.

She arrived in St Ives in March 1940 about six months after Hepworth, Nicholson and Gabo. Apart from periodic forays north of the border she has lived and worked there ever since. In 2001 she received a CBE. Her incisive mind continues to inform her equally incisive and pellucid brush strokes.

LELANT

Lelant ('sacred enclosure of St Anta') churchyard is partly bounded by the West Cornwall Golf Club and overlooks the estuary where the Hayle River yields its nine and a half mile identity into St Ives Bay.

Here is the final resting place of one of Cornwall's most gifted and restive sons, Peter Lanyon, artist and Bard of the Cornish Gorsedd.

A slate slab horizontally embedded in granite, with fine cursive script, bestows a dignified and simple elegance to his grave. A crack running down the length of this slate provides almost perfect symmetry and there is a suspicion that this was caused by a wayward golfing projectile. The following incident is for those cynics who would scoff at this notion.

While seated near this very spot, on a warm summer's afternoon lost in elegiac reverie, I was joined by a plump rabbit also partaking of the idyll. When suddenly one of the aforementioned missiles jolted us from our meditation and your dearly beloved author came within inches of having his skull, with its delicate, refined, cultivated and modest contents (including a gestating *Zawn Lens*), brutally violated!

This lethal object now acts as a *memento mori* on my desk.

SILENT FLIGHT

Another homage, this time for Peter Lanyon (1918–1964).

Speed and danger were a part of Lanyon's make up. But it was the skies that were to be his undoing. Having taken up gliding in 1959, he became highly proficient and was flying solo by the time of his accident.

On August 27 1964, at Dunker's Well aerodrome in Somerset, he took off in bad weather. Conditions proved difficult and he soon attempted a return to base. He came in to land too fast and a wrong move with the rudder resulted in a crash which hurled him out of the cockpit.

Lanyon survived with a cracked vertebra. In hospital, in Taunton, he was typically unsettled, wired up in bed and claiming to know every crack in the ceiling. To everyone's dismay he died, without warning, on August 31 from a blood clot. Lanyon is from the Cornish *lyn yeyn* 'cold pool'.

ZAWN

Zawn is a west Cornwall dialect word derived from the late Cornish *sawan* meaning chasm or cleft. It relates to the Welsh *safn* – mouth or jaw and the Breton *saon* – valley.

A zawn appears as a deep, narrow fissure in the cliffs where the sea has eroded a softer mineral, usually tin, from the harder rock on either side.

This is often quite clear on a map; when it isn't, it is probably the case that more of the cliff has fallen into the sea since the name was given.

Some of the names are clearly linked to mining (*Zawn a Bal*), folklore (*Chough Zawn*) or obvious topological features (*Arch Zawn*); the shape of a feature can be given a metaphorical rendering (*Horseback Zawn*). But there are names whose connotations and associations are well and truly lost (*Cornelias Zawn*).

The following are all the zawns, mainly recorded on the OS 1:25000 map, for the Land's End peninsula, with an *attempt* at giving some of their meanings. Warning: such is the current state of Cornish studies that there is a good deal of inconsistency in spellings; in a few years from now much of this list may well be in need of serious revision!

They are recorded in anti–clockwise order (i.e. starting at St Ives):

Zawn Quoits – quoit is actually an English word for a flat stone or dolmen, plenty of which litter the Cornish moors, but there is also a Cornish word *coyt*, with the same sound and meaning.

Cornelias Zawn – a Christian or surname?

Horseback Zawn – from the shape

Zawn Duel – dark chasm, from *tewl*

Great Zawn

Enys Zawn – island chasm, near The Enys

Trewellard Zawn – near the Trewellard estate

Zawn Brinny – crows' chasm, from *brini*

Levant Zawn – near Levant mine

Boscregan Zawn – dwelling by a small barrow, from *bos* – dwelling, and *creeg* – barrow

Cockle Zawn – named after the shellfish

Stamps & Jowl Zawn – chasm by the Devil's stamping mill, anglicised from
stampez an jowl

Whealcock Zawn – named after Wheal Cock mine

De Narrow Zawn – pennies chasm, anglicised from *dynerow*

Zawn a Bal – chasm by the mine, from *bal* – mine (*wheal* means 'works', and
has gradually come to mean 'mine' but always in conjunction with a name)

Wheal Edward Zawn – near Wheal Edward mine

North Zawn

South Zawn

Zawn Buzz & Gen – chasm by the giant's dwelling, from *Bos an gean*; a good
example of the cartographer's phonetic spelling of a word as it is heard

Castle Zawn – near Maen Castle

Greeb Zawn – reef chasm, from *cryb*

Zawn Wells – grass chasm, from *gwels*

Zawn Trevilley – near Trevilley Cliff or estate

Zawn Pyg – pointed beak chasm

Zawn Peggy – plural of *pyg*

Zawn Reeth – red chasm (previously *Zawn Marhak* – horseman's chasm, 1580)

Zawn Kellys – hidden chasm

Polostoc Zawn – fox's chasm, from *lostoc* – tail, old slang for fox

Chough Zawn – the chough is an emblem for Cornwall (legend has it that the
soul of King Arthur inhabits a chough)

Zawn Gamper – confluence chasm, where currents meet

Zawn Organ – pennyroyal chasm

Long Zawn

Arch Zawn

Zawn Susan – ?

Trequean Zawn – near Trequean farm

My three indispensable books for Cornish place-names are:

O. J. Padel – *Cornish Place-Name Elements*

P. A. S. Pool – *The Place-Names of West Penwith*

Craig Weatherhill – *Cornish Place Names & Language*

BRYAN WYNTER
& THE CARN

It can just about be seen from the road near Eagles Nest. It can also be spotted from the high Trewey Hill road between Zennor and Lady Downs. If the day is clear enough, and binoculars will certainly help, it can be seen from the mid-point of the St Ives to Zennor coastal path. But you have to know what it is before you recognise it.

It is the chimney of The Carn cottage (spelt *Carne* on the OS map). It takes its name from the Cornish *carn* meaning 'rock-pile'. In this instance the name implies its excellent camouflage, the chimney acting as a kind of periscope or turret emerging from the surrounding litter of massive boulders.

The deeds for The Carn cottage go back to 1804 but it is probably older and will surely have been an abode linked to mining and quarrying.

It is located 237m above sea level, with the Logan Stone just to the west and Zennor Quoit to the south-east. It is most conveniently reached by foot on a half-mile track that leads off from the crest of the main road.

To this day it has a sinister reputation amongst the locals. The fact that it is hidden and isolated from the rest of the community has prompted stories of hauntings and witchcraft. These stories had been partially endorsed by the presence of the 'Great Beast' Aleister Crowley, who visited briefly in the '30s. He is supposed to have conjured up the Devil himself in the cottage and performed a black mass down the hill in Zennor's church.

There was also an unfortunate episode at The Carn when Ka Arnold-Foster (the wife of Will Arnold-Foster, a founder member of The League of Nations, who then lived at Eagles Nest and created its outstanding garden) went up there to comfort the ill wife of the writer Gerald Vaughan.

The following morning Mrs Vaughan was found quite mad while Mrs Arnold-Foster was quite dead.

Sydney Graham, who stayed here for 3 months in 1950, referred to the druidical moor of rocks and said 'Christ knows what has been done in the name of magic and worship'.

It is worth noting, however, that this 'mythology' of The Carn, which intrigues people today did not deter families from settling in the vicinity and living undisturbed lives.

It is also very difficult for us to imagine that this austere environment was once well inhabited with large groups of people involved in mining, quarrying, farming and fishing.

The latter two were still important when Bryan Wynter, on his motorbike, arrived in the area immediately after VE day in May 1945.

Wynter, a Londoner, was a pacifist and had spent the war as a registered conscientious objector, working with ditching gangs on land drainage in Oxfordshire and looking after laboratory animals. He now turned to an outlying edge of civilisation for a fresh start; he stayed on in Cornwall for the remaining 30 years of his life.

There was no plumbing or electricity in The Carn but Wynter had an inventive and industrious temperament. Rainwater was collected in a tank from the roof and fed through pipes into the cottage, while a wind generator supplied 12 volts. This was later replaced by a diesel generator. It was not unusual at this time to use paraffin fuelled lamps, irons and cookers.

A small vegetable plot was made and if visitors were lucky they could expect the treat of Algerian wine (a cheap tipple at the time) with the occasional 'luxury' of gull's eggs, secured by Wynter with much risk from fairly inaccessible nesting places. They could also expect a greeting from the tamed raven, Doom. The ambience of these harsh moors clearly had a deep resonance for Wynter. There is often a forlorn orchestration of sound as the wind plays its way through the cracks and crevices in the rocks. The geological formations with their shifting shadows elicit strong reactions from the subconscious of the human observer, particularly at dusk. These rocks definitely have varied character and there is a heavy sense of brooding as if they are giants petrified and slumbering, patiently waiting for that final call to awaken.

Then again there are many days when nothing at all can be seen for the mist. Standing on Zennor Hill I have sometimes seen this mist rapidly approaching and it can be a startling experience to be suddenly engulfed in a cloud and lose your bearings.

Wynter was a much liked man. His death evoked several elegies, most famously from his dear friend Sydney Graham, but also from David Wright, Arthur Caddick and Sven Berlin. He was a social animal and enjoyed the local pubs as well as occasional sorties to London. However, these remote, untamed surroundings continued to be some kind of essential anchor for a more elemental, primordial level of his being as an artist.

Remote though The Carn was, Wynter did not always have to venture out into the art world as the art world also came to him. Apart from the many fellow painters, sculptors and writers in West Penwith there were some very illustrious visitors indeed. In 1958 Mark Rothko and his wife, in cosmopolitan attire, found their way up the dirt track guided by Peter Lanyon; the critics Lawrence Alloway and Clement Greenberg too.

Around 1954 he responded to a newspaper discussion about mescaline which led to him partaking in experiments with the psychical researcher Rosalind Heywood. This exploration of inner space resulted in the use of much larger canvasses and an explosive use of shimmering colour. Wynter seemed to be subconsciously mapping, onto canvas, the lively dance between the workings of his enhanced nervous system with the enriched dimensions of his environment. His wiry, lanky physique appeared to be embodied in the brush strokes as in a distinctive signature. You can get lost in the deep space of these paintings – Patrick Heron said that it felt as if you could shoot an arrow into them.

In the summer of 1957 he built a studio extension himself, with some help from a neighbour, transporting the wooden sections up the track on his Land Rover.

It was Bill Redgrave who gave Wynter part of an old wartime searchlight (a large parabolic mirror). This nagged away at his fertile imagination and over a period of time the IMOOS (images moving out onto space) were gradually born. These consisted of different shapes of painted card suspended in front of the mirror which give the impression of ever shifting, strange and elegant patterns floating in the space ahead of the observer (it was the necessity of exhibiting in a gallery context that dictated the later box format). About a dozen of these were constructed over the next few years, each of them offering a unique illusion; Sven Berlin called them 'timeless clocks'. This kinetic art was a sensible extension from the painting. There is no 'still life' in Wynter, for him the world is forever in flux. Hence his keen interest in what we would now call hydro-dynamics, water being the most potent visual example of dynamic motion.

There was an occasion when the Wynters, going away on a trip, stored a mattress in the studio, where it was less damp. On their return the mattress resembled a huge charcoal biscuit! One of these mirrors, acting as a giant magnifying glass, had each day been focussing the early morning sun on it, leaving it totally charred.

Fire was another element to feature in Wynter's work. Annually, between

January and March, farmers would burn areas of gorse in a controlled way to allow new grass to grow for rough grazing. This was always an exciting, and sometimes intimidating, event. There were some worrying occurrences when the fires got threateningly close to the cottages on the moors and twenty four hour vigilance was called for.

Wynter had married Monica Harman in 1959 (his first marriage was to Susan Lethbridge, who was a toy maker in St Ives). They were to have two boys, Tom in '61 and Billy in '62. In keeping with a self-sufficient ethos, assisted by midwives, a resilient Monica gave birth to these children in The Carn.

Intimations of mortality first came knocking on Bryan Wynter's door in May 1961 when, one night, he had a serious heart attack. Monica ran down the track to the Heron household at Eagles Nest to phone for help. Dr Roger Slack soon arrived in a Land Rover which could negotiate the track, whereas the ambulance couldn't, and this was how the patient was transported to the road.

He spent nearly three months recovering in the Edward Hain hospital in St Ives. It just so happened that one of Wynter's great contemporaries, Tony O'Malley, also had a serious heart attack and ended up in the next bed. Wynter said that O'Malley regaled him with endless stories, never once repeating himself. They were to remain close friends.

Wynter was also fascinated by another, quite different patient. A young man, who had been badly burned while making his own fireworks, provided Wynter with the potent recipe for their concoction. Not long after release from hospital this information was applied to characteristically mischievous practice.

For some time the peace of the moors was regularly shattered by low flying helicopters on exercise drills from RNAS Culdrose. Patrick Heron reported that they flew so low they disturbed the gravel on his drive. Wynter saw a tactical opportunity to experiment with the 'fireworks'. The mixture included weed killer and sugar, the home-made rockets completed with bamboo sticks. Very soon this modest but very effective arsenal was seeing off the invaders. It wasn't long before the RNAS (coincidentally?) sought out an alternative area for their noisy routines.

Swimming, snorkelling and kayaking had always been regular pursuits (not just in Cornwall but also Spain and Ireland, O'Malley once accompanying them on an Irish trip). Wynter, having been impressed by a Jacques Cousteau film, made his own aqualung. A glass bottomed boat was also constructed so that the flowing forms of underwater marine life with attendant eddies, vortices and currents (another kind of deep space) could be studied. These were much featured in the large later paintings.

In 1964 Wynter moved with the family to the more substantial and comfortable Treverven House south of St Buryan.

On February 9 1975 he was working there on changing the punctured wheel of his Mini when he had another heart attack. The fourteen years since the first attack had been very busy and creative and Wynter seemed to have survived again, but was to die in hospital in Penzance two days later.

Bryan Wynter was a non-partisan man in the sometimes combative and jealous world of art politics. He was extremely popular and in speaking to people who knew him the same word recurs – *gentle*. Peter Lanyon said 'he was a very generous human being but remained anonymous with it'. He was a literary man widely read in poetry, philosophy and the sciences. A romantic who, in a significant way, managed to bridge the often yawning gap of 'the two cultures', the traditional schism between art and science.

A simple stone marks his grave in Zennor churchyard. The stone was taken from the old count house on his beloved moors just east of The Carn where he had lived, loved and worked for 19 years.

Tony O'Malley

Unedited version of The Guardian *obituary (April 11 2003)*

The Irish painter Tony O'Malley, who has died aged 89, was an important player in the St Ives art community between 1960 and 1990. But his high place in Irish art of the 20th century, along with Jack Yeats, Patrick Collins and Louis le Brocquy, is by now well established.

O'Malley was born in Callan, Co. Kilkenny, in 1913. His genealogy can be traced back to notorious stock from Clare Island, Co. Mayo. The 16th century pirate Grace O'Malley amongst them. His father Patrick was a salesman for Singer Sewing Machines; his mother, Margaret Ryan, came from the town.

He first attended the convent school, followed by the local Christian Brothers.

O'Malley's earliest exposure to art was mainly to be found in the stone carvings of nearby abbeys, particularly the late-Gothic work of Rory O'Tunney. They remained a lasting influence.

At the age of 19 he got a job as a bank clerk in the Munster & Leinster Bank and, with the exception of a year in the Irish Army in 1940, this remained his employment for 25 years. His health throughout this period was atrocious. It included TB with a stay in a sanatorium. For solace he painted: still-life, landscape and self portraits (the latter a lifelong obsession). He was on a steep learning curve, the influence of van Gogh and Cezanne being clear; nevertheless there are many striking paintings including *Mines, Avoca* (1952) and *Portrait of my Mother* (1953).

In 1955 he visited St Ives in Cornwall on a painting vacation. He could hardly have chosen a more exciting, fertile and dynamic place for a burgeoning artist. The small harbour town boasted an embarrassment of riches with many of the finest artists of post-war years living and working there or nearby. They included Barbara Hepworth, Wilhelmina Barns-Graham, Peter Lanyon, Bryan Wynter, Patrick Heron, John Wells, Roger Hilton, Terry Frost, Bernard Leach and the poet Sydney Graham.

The stimulation of this bright, energetic and inventive ambience must have been totally exhilarating to O'Malley coming from the suffocating and guilt ridden Catholic Ireland of the '50s. He soon gave up the day job.

In 1960 O'Malley set sail from Ireland on the cattle boat and settled in West Cornwall for the next 30 years. In 1961 he had a serious heart attack and ended up in hospital in St Ives, coincidentally in the next bed to Bryan Wynter who had also had a heart attack. Wynter later said that O'Malley entertained them both with an endless stream of stories, never once repeating himself. He convalesced with the Heron family, an indication of how quickly people felt at ease with him.

This memento of the transience of life acted as a spur to his work and he said 'Illness brings detachment, having escaped being a phantom I delighted in reality'.

(His life can also be read as a medical catalogue of ailments which included TB, with the removal of a lung, several heart attacks, pneumonia and cancer of a toe, which was amputated, a reminder of the old proverb: squeaky doors hang long.)

The 1960s were tremendously creative years for O'Malley. He approached landscape painting in a visceral way akin to his fellow Celt Peter Lanyon, where canvas, board, or any surface for that matter was scored and ingrained, reflecting the harshness of the local sea, granite and gorse environment.

Bernard Leach introduced him to an Oriental aesthetic where all material, regardless of how crude, is deemed worthy of artistic transformation, old newspapers, boxes, driftwood etc. Hence there is often a feeling of roughness or incompleteness about much of the work.

Throughout his career birds were a recurring motif in his work with titles such as *The Hawk Owl*, *Hawk's Landscape*, *Birdsong Cycle*, *The Windhover*, *The Falcon's Gyre*, *The Bird Window*, *Owls Ruling a Wood at Night*, *Jackdaw*.

In his 60th year O'Malley, the inveterate bachelor, surprised those who thought they knew him by quietly getting married to the Canadian painter Jane Harris (then half his age). Thus a whole new phase of his life began. She provided him with a new impetus and focus and encouraged him to travel more widely, particularly to the Bahamas, which subsequently broadened his palette to a much more exuberant use of daring and bright colours. (It is probably safe to say that without Jane this obituary would have been written a good deal earlier.)

In 1990 they returned permanently to Ireland. Back near O'Malley's birthplace, in Physicianstown, they bought a labourer's cottage which they developed making a superb studio space with garden. Typically, as bits of wood were discarded by the builders O'Malley would seize on this 'debris' and lovingly carve and decorate it.

Recent years have brought many honours to Tony O'Malley, including Honorary Membership of the Royal Hibernian Academy, *The Guardian* Art Critic's Award for Painting, an Honorary Doctorate from Trinity College, the freedom of the city of Kilkenny and perhaps the most high profile of all: the honour of *Saoi* (wise man) was conferred on him by members of *Aosdana*. For this he was presented with a *torc* (a spiral necklace) by President Mary Robinson, the previous holder of this particular award being Samuel Beckett.

Recently the Taylor Galleries in Dublin held a 50 year retrospective of his work, which contained over 160 paintings and coincided with a show of new graphic work shared with Jane. His output has always been prolific. This had nothing to do with ambition, his need to make art everyday was as simple as his need to breathe; he had an urge to catch the moment.

In Cornwall O'Malley is recalled with enormous affection. He was an uncomplicated man who played no part in political rivalries, though he was also widely read and well informed. As a story teller and singer of ballads he was legendary.

But it is the richly unique visual language that he developed as a self-taught artist that will remain his legacy. He is survived by Jane.

Tony O'Malley, painter, born September 25 1913; died January 20 2003

Peter Lanyon's
Place Oddysey

The stink of cow dung is not usually associated with the hallowed air of a London art gallery, at least not in 1952! But this is what Peter Lanyon claimed to be offering to the London dealers Gimpel Fils, in the form of 'concentrated essence of farmyard', while painting *Bojewyan Farms*. Stimulating the eyesight alone of the senses gave Lanyon little satisfaction as an artist.

Not content to paint a representation of what he saw he ventured to paint his very *act* of seeing. Seeing engaged the total body in the multi-sensual experience of *being in a place*. In this case a very rural farm setting between Morvah and Pendeen.

As a boy Lanyon explored the Cornish landscape on horseback – one of the early modes of transport he was to incorporate in his attempts to actively connect with a place. The horse was to reappear in later years in various paintings including *Blue Horse Truant* (1945), *The Yellow Runner* (1946) and finally in one of his own poems, part of which is carved on his gravestone.

Lanyon was also to employ bicycles, cars and gliders to amplify the various physical sensations of moving in space, offering him new ways to experience and gain familiarity with his environment.

He always had a yearning to be a racing driver. Fast cars, or at least cars driven fast, were a passion not always shared by his passengers on twisty Cornish roads!

His first brief experience of flight was at the end of the war. Having joined the RAF in 1940, it was ironic, in view of his subsequent experience, that he was excluded from pilot training because of migraine. Instead, he served as an aero-engine fitter in five different countries including Egypt, Palestine and Italy.

Even before the final gliding phase of his life Lanyon endeavoured to undermine the single, static perspective approach to landscape painting by various processes of disorientation. He constantly tried to subvert habits of perception. The body in motion, particularly in some dangerous adventures on the edge of cliffs, provided a heightened awareness of the dynamic interplay of the artist with his surroundings. The landscape ceased to be *in* space but *was* space. (Gabo's perspex constructions proved to be a lasting influence on Lanyon.) The painting itself was not a flat surface but was endowed with a depth that drew the viewer in at the same time the painting 'entered' the viewer, thus encouraging a circular participation of the observer with the observed (Wynter's work of the late '50s had a similar effect).

These were not mere academic exercises in the philosophy of space.

They were given a solid grounding in the specificity of a venue or situation. The first place we find ourselves is our bodies; not in, but as a body coupling with an environment. A body moving in space and time, *paying attention*, generates the experience of a place. Lanyon certainly paid attention. He did drawings and rapid sketches on location and collected material for assembling his constructions which then activated his memory, as a three dimensional mnemonic, of being in the place (he said 'hands making an object release meaning'). His sensuous exposure to various places, which included particular weather conditions, or the sudden startled flight of a bird and history (Lanyon was a proud Cornishman and was acutely aware of the millennia of his forebears' activity in this seemingly wild, untamed terrain) were all captured as moments in time. Paintings took many months of intense labour and what sometimes appeared to be finished proved to be yet another layer in the process of its evolution. Lanyon's work is a form of excavation in that, paradoxically, as he adds he digs deeper. The finished product is not 'abstract' in that word's definition of being a theoretical idea removed from material experience, but is in fact a highly tactile embodiment of his being in a place. This was visionary topography.

The titles of Lanyon's works are particularly evocative of the Cornish land, sea and skyscape he thrived in. He made lists of these names and agonised over them for months, in some cases years (*St Just*). It makes an interesting kind of cartographic inventory to divide some of these titles into specific place-names; unspecified place; weather and activity (my categories are of course arbitrary, as places, weather and activity often overlap).

A Folly

As fine an example of the genus of folly that you are likely to meet.

From the road between Nancledra and Badger's Cross, looking west, can be seen, almost dreamlike, what looks like a toy fort. This building is known as Roger's or Rogers' Tower, built about 1798. (It is not known whether Roger is a first name or a surname.) Whoever Roger or Rogers was he is now considered, by archaeologists, to have been a vandal. From the adjacent iron age fort of Castle-an-Dinas (this is a translingual tautology, *dinas* being the Cornish for fort or castle) our mysterious Roger cannibalised the stonework for his ostentatious fabrication, ruining the ancient ruins to build a more modern ruin. What for?

Borlase's contention that this was a gothic privy, a convenience for the unbridled traveller, though accepted without question for more than a century, no longer holds water, so to speak. To be fair to Borlase he never did commit this notion to parchment but was heard to conjecture as much late one evening in the nearby Sheep Shearer's Arms, having downed a number of flagons of the local steam brew. Apparently he had put his hypothesis to the test, with regularity, without fail. (Alas this infamous hostelry is no longer an inn but is yet *another* pottery selling cream teas.)

It also goes without saying that the Borlase in question here was not the renowned antiquary and naturalist Dr William Borlase (1696–1772), but Ebenezer Obadiah Borlase who hailed from Hayle. A distant cousin of the esteemed doctor (diligent research, by a team of Peruvian academics, suggests he was at least 37 times removed), his aspirations to scholarship have at times fostered controversy. His lifelong dedication to the notion that herds of wild albino elephants once rampaged across West Penwith, using the antiquities as rump scratchers, hence their state of disrepair, and lived in fogous – undergound chambers – was typical of an obsessive bent of mind. His detailed account of fogous as an ideal environment for this unique species of Cornish elephant during their mating season, published as three large volumes of *Cornubia Archaeologia*, has, unfortunately, been lost without trace. Indeed this led to that notoriously shameful episode at The Union Hotel in Penzance. It was at an extraordinary meeting of the Grumbla Fogou Club, in the Lady

Hamilton Suite, when most ungentlemanly fisticuffs resulted in the indecorous defacing of a bust of Viscount Horatio Nelson no less (i.e., he got a chipped hooter). Having said all that, his notion that Lanyon Quoit was a kind of neolithic coffee table indicating that the inhabitants of the region were once much, much, much taller has yet to be disproved.

But we digress. Gadzooks! Indeed we do.

Perhaps the purpose of a folly is that it doesn't have a purpose. It may also be a simple fact that, in this instance, the 'architect' was crack-brained, to use a charming contemporary term (or to phrase it with post-modernist acumen: *he was two sausages short of a full mixed grill*), *ergo* with no rationale required.

Though we may no longer see the point of Roger's erection, suggesting mild delusions of grandeur, we can still take our pleasure from it as a harmless sham of a bygone age when it was folly to be wise.

Lanyon Quoit frames Ding Dong Mine (Greenburrow Shaft)

CONCLUDING
INTRODUCTION

It was the melted end of that most melting of summers.

September 1976 was when I first visited Cornwall on holiday. Why, I can no longer remember. I travelled by coach from London to St Ives and pitched my tent at Hellesveor Farm on the edge of town.

I knew nothing about Cornwall, Cornish art, literature or history. In fact, generally speaking, I knew nothing about almost everything.

I set about exploring the area on foot and by bus.

I remember walking to Zennor, on the road, wearing some cheap sandals that made my feet sweat more than if I'd been wearing gum boots! I arrived parched and would have killed for a drink but the pub was closed. I recall getting some refreshment at the Wayside Museum before returning across the fields over the stiles.

I also visited the newly-opened Barbara Hepworth Garden and Museum. Needless to say I'd never heard of her, but this was my introduction to the modernist art movement that so interests me today. In fact looking around St Ives I was most taken by the art and craft on show in the little galleries. There was a strange nameless quality that seemed to relate to the immediate environment.

One day I took the bus to Porthcurno and went for an amble along the coastal path. What I stumbled across astonished me: a classical amphitheatre carved from the almost sheer cliff face! In outstanding condition, given the fact that it must have been thousands of years old. Probably the Romans, I surmised. Having marvelled at their engineering prowess I continued on my way.

On the return loop I got lost. In the garden of a large house I noticed an elderly woman pruning a tree and stopped to ask directions. There was something most striking about her appearance, she blended in with the blasted trees and hedges of her surroundings with her lean sinewy limbs and weathered complexion. She had a charismatic elemental presence. I mentioned the 'ancient' theatre on the cliffs. She looked taken aback and said that she had built it herself! With the help of friends and volunteers, over several decades, she had hauled sack loads of sand from the beach far below (hence her elongated arms) to create the eighth wonder of the world: the Minack Theatre. (At this time the theatre was totally *open* to cliff walkers, unlike today where it now resembles Colditz.) We chatted about various things including her diet, which consisted mainly of honey. I left her, feeling I had met a remarkable human being. It was many years later before I discovered that I had met the legendary Rowena Cade (1893–1983).

Not all of this trip proved as pleasantly memorable. One evening in St Ives I was forced, by a shocking storm, to stay for several hours against my will in The Sloop Inn. When I eventually got back to the campsite my tent and its contents were not to be found: they had been blown over the edge of a nearby cliff (and were last seen passing the Azores at a rate of knots). I spent the night on the floor of the communal lavatory (a once in a lifetime experience – I hope) and the following morning I reluctantly got the coach back to London.

But I had been touched and enchanted by an inexpressible magic, that strange nameless quality of Cornwall and in particular West Penwith. I will return, I thought, I will certainly return ...

Haiku Coda

Nervous gulls cluster,
Salt-laden lips pursed against
The razor windsea

SUBSCRIBERS

I am humbly indebted to the following people whose fiscal faith
helped to kick-start the publication of this book:

Janet Axten – St Ives, Cornwall
Wilhelmina Barns-Graham – St Ives, Cornwall
Jan Beare – Newmill, Cornwall
Vanilla Beer – Esperaza, France
Richard Budd – Merriott, Somerset
Diana (née Caddick) & Ken Calvert – Northam, Devon
Jon Carpenter – Finstock, Oxon
Brian Carter – Deddington, Oxon
Dell Casdagli – St Ives, Cornwall
Jonathan Clark – Chelsea, London
Ursula & James Cornish – Camden, London
Douglas Cook – Ding Dong, Cornwall
David Alban Davies – Chipping Norton, Oxon
Peter & Budge English – Ruthin, Wales
Eleanor Edwards – Ascott-Under-Wychwood, Oxon
Peter Evans – St Ives, Cornwall
Edward Fenton – Charlbury, Oxon
Sue Fuller – Old Marston, Oxford
Hilary & George Gandy – Charlbury, Oxon
Sir Scott Grant – Charlbury, Oxon
Melissa Hardie – Newmill, Cornwall
Derek & Rosomond Hyatt – Wetherby, Yorkshire
Dave Jacobs – Battersea, London
Joy & Ray Kell – Gurnard's Head, Cornwall
Andrew Lawson – Charlbury, Oxon
Tracy Le Cornu – Chelsea, London
John Oldham – Ramsden, Oxon
Edward Richardson – Cumnor, Oxford
Toby Ridge – Winchester, Hants
Neville Shack – Kensington, London
Dr Roger Slack – St Ives, Cornwall
Sarah Stoten – Shipston-on-Stour, Warwickshire
David Tobin – Camden, London
Robert Twigger – Summertown, Oxford
Alan Ward – Wadham College, Oxford
Simon Whitehead – Charlbury, Oxon
David Kim Whittaker – St Ives, Cornwall (no relation!)
Bob Wilkins – Charlbury, Oxon
Ges Wilson – Penzance, Cornwall
Sue Wilson – Zennor, Cornwall
Wendy Wilson – Charlbury, Oxon
Monica Wynter – Penzance, Cornwall